CONTENTS

INTRODUCTION

My life has been a series of food moments, made mostly at home. I grew up in a family where we did nothing but eat, drink and entertain – and therefore, that is what I aspired to do. The door was always open, a sauce was continuously simmering on the stove and the libations were flowing. You got me; I'm a lush in chef's clogs. Can you blame me?

Over the years I've built a career teaching "foodies" essential skills to elevate and inspire their home cooking. But it's important to recognize that cooking at home is more than just food. Everyday food and entertaining is what people remember. This sentiment towards the ordinary celebrations is what originally and continually motivates me. After all, **simple food is at the heart of everyday entertaining.**

The first thing chefs are taught is the importance of seasoning, tasting and balancing flavors. But you don't need a culinary degree to learn the secret to create swoon-worthy meals for your friends and family. **Thoughtful, well-prepared food is delicious because of two things: acid and salt. Or shall I say, lemon & salt.**

The inspiration behind this book grew from a superficial reason: my friends needed to learn how to cook. I was tired of being everyone's "chef" friend. But it was bigger than that, there were no cookbooks for the "modern girl." The female equivalents of Peter Pan, filled with boozy brunches (page 63) and date nights (page 17). Women living alone, with roommates, newly married or starting families that are working too hard, for too little and just not … cooking. Onion to pan, knife to board, grocery store to mouth.

Ironically, these women consider themselves foodies. They are talking, reading, writing, blogging and eating – but not cooking. Why aren't they cooking?!

This cookbook is designed for women who admire the traditional role of their grandmothers in the kitchen, fantasize of a Pinterest-ed "Dream Kitchen" but live with the realities of limited time, money or space. *Lemon & Salt* teaches approachable techniques in a use-what-you-have mentality.

These 50+ recipes are unfussy, practical and memorable. From lunching to tailgating, **be bold in your kitchen revelry.** My hope is for this cookbook to help you **define and embrace your everyday celebrations in the kitchen.**

Ashton Keefe

Tips for Kitchen Revelry

1. **You can cook, stop saying you can't.** If you can recognize something on a menu and you have hands to hold a knife, you got this. Trust me.

2. **Make it as complicated (or uncomplicated) as you want.** There are short cuts to make your life easier and classic techniques to step up your game – chefs at home use both, daily. No judgment.

3. **You won't break the bank** with ingredients (all recipes contain minimal ingredients – many of them repeatable!). You don't need a big fancy kitchen or specialty equipment.

4. Go easy on yourself, it's supposed to be fun. It's the **thought**, **experience** and **people** you share a meal with that make it memorable.

5. **Cooking is significantly more fun (and easier) when wine is involved.** Just saying.

Cheers!

P.S. Follow @ashtonkeefe and tag **#lemonandsalt** on Instagram to share your culinary revelries.

rev · el · ry, noun
lively and noisy festivities, especially when these involve drinking a large amount of alcohol

weeknight meals

The go-to meals when you're in a hurry and need to depend on pantry staples. This isn't a special occasion, it's an everyday occasion and it's the hardest one to tackle.

CHICKEN AND BISCUITS

———

MUSTARD ROASTED SALMON & PEA SMASH

———

PORK TENDERLOIN WITH SQUASH POLENTA

———

ONE PAN CHICKEN

———

TURKEY MEATBALLS

———

DATE NIGHT: CARBONARA

Chicken and Biscuits
MAKES ONE LARGE CASSEROLE

The most wonderful part of this recipe is that it can be as simple or complex as you want. Feel like roasting your own chicken? Go for it. Opting for a store-bought rotisserie chicken? Even easier. Biscuit making scare you? Or don't have a food processor? Buy store-bought biscuit dough or simply cover with thawed puff pastry from your grocery's freezer section. No judgment here.

Casserole

1 tablespoon extra virgin olive oil
1 large yellow onion, diced
2 large carrots, peeled and chopped
1 celery rib, chopped
1 pound shiitake mushrooms, stemmed and thinly sliced
1 cup dry white wine
2 tablespoons unsalted butter
2 tablespoons all-purpose flour
2 - 3 cups low sodium chicken broth
Fine sea salt, to taste
1 small chicken, roasted and shredded
1 bunch kale, de-ribbed and thinly sliced

Biscuit Crumb Topping

2 cups all-purpose flour
1 teaspoon salt
1 teaspoon baking soda
1 teaspoon baking powder
4 tablespoons unsalted butter, cubed and chilled
2 tablespoons chopped sage
Zest of 1 lemon
1/2 cup whole milk

Preheat the oven to 425° F.

In a large Dutch oven sauté onion, carrot, celery and mushroom over medium heat, stirring, until vegetables are softened, about 8 minutes. Add wine and "deglaze" (aka, scrape the brown bits off the bottom of) the pan. Cook until the wine evaporates, about 1 minute.

Push all vegetables to the side of the pan and add butter to the open part of the pan. Stir in the 2 - 3 tablespoons of flour and whisk for one minute until the flour is slightly browned. Add broth to the flour mixture to create a roux and whisk to eliminate lumps. Stir until thick and creamy, about 5 minutes. Season with salt. Stir in the vegetables from the side of the pan to combine. Add chicken and kale. Leave in the Dutch-oven or transfer to a buttered casserole dish.

In a food processor, combine all dry ingredients and butter, pulse until butter is the size of peas. Add milk and again pulse, just until a crumble forms.

Place crumble over chicken and bake for 12 - 15 minutes until casserole is bubbling and biscuit top is golden.

Roasted Mustard and Herb Salmon with Pea Smash
SERVES 8

This is the dinner you make when company spontaneously shows up. And since salmon is everyone's favorite (and go-to) fish, this is a perfect, pantry-driven weeknight meal. I call this "kitchen sink" fish. It tastes better than it sounds – I promise. It simply means use whatever herbs and mustards you have on hand. Frozen peas should be a freezer staple for everyone. Don't tell, but they're easier (and taste the same) as the shucked ones come spring. P.S. This tastes great with a nice white wine. Now that's an impromptu Tuesday party.

Salmon
1 shallot, minced
1 cup chopped parsley
1/2 cup chopped chives
1/2 cup chopped dill
4 scallions, green and white parts, chopped
Juice and zest of 1 lemon
1/4 cup Dijon mustard
1/4 cup whole grain mustard
1/4 cup extra virgin olive oil
2 teaspoons fine sea salt, divided
2 lbs. salmon, skin on

Pea Smash

1/2 cup heavy cream, chicken broth or water
1 10 ounce bag of frozen peas, thawed
2 tablespoons unsalted butter
Fine sea salt, to taste

Remove salmon from the refrigerator 30 minutes before roasting.

Preheat the oven to 425° F.

Combine shallot, parsley, chives, dill, scallions, lemon juice and zest, mustards and olive oil. Stir to combine and season with 1 teaspoon of salt.

On a parchment lined sheet tray place whole fish skin side down. Season with remaining teaspoon of salt and slather the spread on the top of the fish.

Cook for 10 - 12 minutes or until fish is firm and falls apart when touched, but not dry in the center.

For smash bring your choice of liquid to a simmer, add peas and cook until the liquid is just evaporated. With a fork smash peas to desired texture, add butter and season with salt Serve under salmon.

Make the smash skinnier or more indulgent by choosing between heavy cream, milk, chicken broth or water as your liquid.

This recipe also works with frozen corn and edamame.

Tip: Smaller crowd? Make the spread as is and freeze extra. Or, use as a salad dressing or pesto by adding more olive oil.

Mustard Pork Tenderloin and Squash Polenta
SERVES 4

Pork really is the new white meat. I'd argue that pork tenderloin is this decade's boneless chicken breast – but tastier. What I love about this recipe is that it replicates the flavors of my favorite guilty pleasure, a hot dog, but in a healthier way.

Polenta

1 acorn squash, quartered and seeded
1 tablespoons extra virgin olive oil, divided
2 teaspoons fine sea salt, divided
1/2 teaspoon freshly cracked black pepper
2 cups water, milk, cream or broth
1/2 cup uncooked dry polenta, not instant
2 tablespoons unsalted butter

Pork

1 pork tenderloin, excess fat trimmed
1 tablespoons extra virgin olive oil
1 1/2 teaspoons fine sea salt, divided
1 shallot, minced
1 tablespoon honey
2 tablespoons whole grain mustard
2 tablespoons Dijon mustard
1/2 cup hazelnuts, toasted and chopped
Maldon sea salt, optional

Preheat oven to 400° F.

On a parchment lined sheet tray place squash skin side down and sprinkle with 1 tablespoon olive oil, 1 teaspoon salt and pepper. Place in the oven.

Heat 1 tablespoon olive oil in an ovenproof skillet over medium high heat. Pat the pork dry with paper towels and season with 1 teaspoon salt. Sear pork 3 - 4 minutes per side, until browned. Remove pan from the heat and leave pork in the pan.

Mix remaining 1/2 teaspoon salt, shallot, honey and mustards together. Slather on the pork and place in the oven. Finish cooking for 15 - 20 minutes or until the internal temperature of the pork reaches 145° F. Remove pork from the pan and tent with tin foil.

At about the same time, the squash will be tender. Remove from the oven and spoon out flesh into a bowl and mash with the back of a fork until puree-like.

Bring water (or choice liquid) to a boil and slowly whisk in polenta until it begins to thicken. Add squash puree, butter and remaining teaspoon of salt. Keep warm.

Serve polenta under pork and garnish with hazelnuts and Maldon.

Tip: Polenta can vary in consistency. To make consistency tighter, use less liquid. And vise versa.

One Pan Chicken

SERVES 4

I love this recipe. To me, the aroma of roast chicken symbolizes home, family and love. What's even better is that ingredients can be substituted for shallots, lemon and garlic. Or make it a party and invite all the ingredients – and your friends.

1 - 2 tablespoons extra virgin olive oil
2 teaspoons fine sea salt
1 2 - 3 lb. chicken, broken into 4 pieces, 2 legs
and 2 breasts
4 cloves garlic, smashed
2 shallots, thinly sliced
1 lemon, thinly sliced
2 tablespoons unsalted butter
1 cup dry white wine
1 bunch chives, finely chopped

En lieu of garlic, shallot, lemon, use ...

- Lime, jalapeno, peppers
- Onion, butternut squash, sage
- Leeks, fennel, Pernod
- Carrots, parsnip, celery
- Peas, corn, zucchini

Preheat oven to 425° F.

Heat olive oil in a large, ovenproof skillet over medium high heat. Pat chicken dry using a paper towel and season with salt. Sear chicken skin side down until golden brown, 4 - 5 minutes. Remove chicken from the pan. Remove the pan from heat.

To the pan add garlic, shallots and lemon. Place chicken skin side up over shallot/lemon mixture and add butter and wine. Place pan in the oven and cook for additional 20 - 25 minutes until the juices run clear and chicken's internal temperature is 165° F.

Garnish with chives.

14

Turkey Meatballs

MAKES 12 MEATBALLS

Simple, healthy and loaded with pantry staples, these meatballs will be your new favorite.

1 tablespoon extra virgin olive oil
1 onion, diced
1 teaspoon dried oregano
1 teaspoon dried red pepper flakes
3 gloves garlic, minced
1 tablespoon tomato paste
2 - 3 tablespoons dry red wine
1 lb. ground turkey meat
1 teaspoon fine sea salt
1 egg
1/2 cup panko bread crumbs
Marinara sauce (page 25)
Parmesan cheese, garnish

In a large skillet heat olive oil over medium heat and sauté onion until translucent, about 5 minutes. Add spices and garlic, cooking until fragrant, about 1 minute. Add tomato paste and cook for an additional minute. Pour in red wine and stir until liquid evaporates.

Remove from heat and allow the onion mixture to cool completely.

In a large bowl combine ground turkey, salt, egg, panko and onion mixture. Mix until ingredients are fully combined. Roll into 12 equal sized balls.

In the pan used to cook the onions, place meatballs and enough marinara sauce to cover the balls. Simmer sauce, turning meatballs as needed until they are cooked through.

Serve with pasta, polenta, in a roll or naked. Garnish with cheese.

Tip: I call dried oregano and red pepper flakes my "pizza parlor" spices, which is both corny and practical. These two spices are in every household and elicit nostalgia for the Italian-American food we all love.

Date Night: Carbonara
SERVES 2

I call Carbonara my "sexy weeknight dinner." It's easy too, which means little clean up – because let's be honest, no one is cleaning up after dinner.

1 lb. bucatini pasta
6 pieces of center cut bacon, chopped
1 onion, diced
3 cloves garlic, minced
2 egg yolks
1 whole egg
1 cup parmesan cheese, plus more for garnish
Zest of 1 lemon
Black pepper, garnish

Bring a large pot of water to a boil and salt generously (it should be as salty as the sea). Cook pasta until al dente. Reserve 1/2 cup pasta water for loosening the sauce.

Meanwhile, sauté bacon over medium heat to render fat and crisp bacon, about 8 minutes. Remove bacon from the pan and set aside on a paper towel to drain excess fat. Leave about 2 tablespoons bacon fat in the pan (reserve extra for something else yummy ...) and sauté onions until caramelized, about 5 minutes. Add garlic and cook until fragrant, about 1 minute. Remove pan from heat.

In a small bowl, whisk eggs, cheese and lemon zest together.

Place hot pasta in the pan and pour egg mixture on top. Use tongs, toss the pasta until creamy. Use reserved pasta water to loosen the sauce if desired.

Portion into two large bowls and top with more cheese and cracked black pepper. Serve with wine.

Tip: This pasta recipe makes extra and doubles as a brunch item (yes!). With bacon, egg and cheese, it is the ultimate hangover cure.

m.y.o.p.

In my family we have a tradition: M.Y.O.P. night. M.Y.O.P. stands for **m**ake **y**our **o**wn **p**izza. You'll love this night so much; pizza delivery will be a thing of the past.

PIZZA DOUGH

———

EVERYDAY MARINARA SAUCE

———

BASIL PESTO

———

THE BEST BOLOGNESE

———

ZUCCHINI BLOSSOM PIZZA

———

HOMEMADE RICOTTA CHEESE

———

MONTANARA PIE

———

GRILLED MUSHROOM FLATBREAD

Classic Pizza Dough
MAKES 3 DOUGHS

What's wonderful about M.Y.O.P. night is that you can make it as simple or do-it-yourself as you'd like. Want to take it to the next level? Try this dough. It's easy, I promise.

4 1/2 cups unbleached bread flour
1 teaspoon instant yeast
1 3/4 teaspoon fine sea salt
1 tablespoon honey
1/4 cup extra virgin olive oil
1 3/4 cup water, approximately 110° F

In a large bowl, whisk flour, yeast and salt.

In a stand mixer fitted with a hook attachment add flour mixture and remaining ingredients, knead on the lowest speed until a ball begins to form, 2 - 3 minutes. Add 1 tablespoon of extra flour as needed if dough seems sticky – adding no more than 3 tablespoons! Continue to knead until the dough is smooth and slightly warm, 5 - 7 minutes longer.

If kneading by hand use a wooden spoon to combine all ingredients. When the dough begins to come together roll out to a floured surface and knead until smooth and slightly warm, about 10 - 12 minutes.

Oil a bowl and place the dough in it. Cover with a towel and allow the dough to rise for 4 hours.

Use immediately, refrigerate for 4 - 5 days or freeze for up to 3 months.

Tip: Two things kill yeast, salt and hot water. To prevent this don't pour salt directly on the yeast when combining ingredients. To avoid water temperatures being too hot, err on the side of cooler water. Cooler water will result in a longer rise period, but work exactly the same.

everyday marinara

basil pesto

Everyday Marinara Sauce

MAKES 2 QUARTS

This sauce is simple, easy and timeless. Minimal ingredients that make a huge impression.

1 tablespoon extra virgin olive oil
1 onion, diced
3 garlic cloves, minced
1 28 ounce can crushed tomatoes
2 teaspoons fine sea salt

Heat olive oil in a large skillet over medium heat. Sauté onion until translucent, about 5 minutes. Add garlic and cook until fragrant, about 1 minute.

Add tomatoes and salt. Simmer and enjoy.

Basil Pesto

MAKES 1 PINT

I like to call pesto "summer in a jar." Don't have basil on hand (or not in season)? Use any bunch of herbs or peppery greens. Parsley, chives, cilantro and arugula all work.

1 bunch basil, leaves only
3 gloves garlic
1/4 cup toasted pine nuts
1/4 cup Parmesan cheese
1 teaspoon fine sea salt
1/2 cup extra virgin olive oil

Combine first five ingredients in a food processor and pulse until the mixture is coarse. With the machine on slowly stream in olive oil.

For a more liquidy pesto use up to 1 cup olive oil.

You can also do this the old-fashioned way with a mortar and pestle.

The Best Beef Bolognese

MAKES 2 QUARTS

Everyone needs a good meat sauce in their back pocket. Italian purists may have a problem with cheese and dairy in this sauce but I think it adds a little something-something. Like a sweeter sauce? Add 1 teaspoon sugar, 1/2 cup chopped roasted red peppers (like my Mom!) or sauté 2 diced carrots with your onion. My favorite ways to eat this sauce include pasta, M.Y.O.P and best of all – on a crusty loaf of bread.

1 tablespoon extra virgin olive oil
1 onion, diced
1 teaspoon dried oregano
1 teaspoon dried red pepper flakes
4 garlic cloves, minced
1 tablespoon tomato paste
1 lb. ground sirloin
1 1/2 teaspoon fine sea salt, more to taste
1/2 bottle dry red wine
1 28 ounce can of crushed tomatoes
1/4 cup heavy cream
1/4 cup grated Parmesan cheese
Freshly grated nutmeg

In a large skillet heat olive oil over medium high heat and sauté onion until translucent, about 5 minutes. Add oregano, pepper flakes, garlic and tomato paste and cook for 1 minute until fragrant. Add meat and brown, breaking up with a wooden spoon. Season with salt.

Add wine and deglaze, scraping the bottom of the pan. Add tomatoes and bring to a boil, reduce to a simmer and cook for 20 minutes.

Add cream, cheese and nutmeg. Season with salt to taste.

Serve over pasta or in a sturdy hoagie roll.

26

beef bolognese

Zucchini Pizza with Stuffed Squash Blossoms
MAKES 1 PIE

This is the *perfect* summer pie. Squash blossoms are available at the farmer's markets mid-July through August, grab them while you can. They are equally delicious stuffed with goat cheese.

1 pizza dough (page 21)
2 tablespoons extra virgin olive oil
1 yellow zucchini, diced
1 green zucchini, diced
1 cup grated Parmesan cheese
1 1/2 teaspoon fine sea salt, divided
4 squash blossoms
4 ounces ricotta cheese (below or store bought)
1 egg, whisked
1 cup all purpose flour

Preheat a large cast iron pan in the oven set at 500° F.

On a floured surface use your hands to work the dough into a 10" - 12" circle. Remove cast iron skillet from the oven and dust with flour. Place shaped dough in the pan and top with 1 tablespoon olive oil, zucchini, Parmesan cheese and 1/2 teaspoon salt. Bake until golden brown and bubbling, about 10 - 12 minutes.

Meanwhile, heat remaining tablespoon olive oil in a skillet over medium high heat. In a small bowl beat egg and season with 1/2 teaspoon salt. In another small bowl add flour and season with remaining 1/2 teaspoon salt.

Gently handling the squash blossoms, stuff each with about 1 tablespoon of ricotta cheese. Lightly dip blossom into egg mixture and then flour mixture. Place in hot oil and sear each side until brown, about 1 minute per side.

Remove pizza from the oven and top with blossoms.

Garnish with additional olive oil or salt.

Fresh Ricotta Cheese
MAKES 1 QUART

Line a colander with a heavy layer of cheesecloth. Bring **1 quart milk** and **1 quart heavy cream** to a simmer over high heat and stir in **2 tablespoons white wine vinegar**. Stir and simmer the mixture for few minutes until curds form, remove from heat. Allow the mixture to rest for 20 minutes. Pour in colander and allow whey (liquid) to drain until desired cheese texture is achieved. Season with **salt**.

Montanara Pie
MAKES 1 PIE

This pizza is fried. Don't worry, it's not greasy. Montanara pie is the original pie of Naples and the result is easier than ever to achieve at home.

1 cup vegetable oil
1 pizza dough (page 21)
1 cup marinara sauce (page 25)
1/4 lb. mozzarella cheese, sliced
1 bunch fresh basil
Fine sea salt, to taste
Olive oil, garnish

Equipment

Deep fryer or deep-sided pan

In a high-sided pot heat oil to 365° F. Preheat broiler.

Shape pizza into a 9" - 10" round and poke the dough with a fork to create small holes. Slide dough into the hot oil and fry for 45 seconds. Flip using tongs and fry the other side for 45 seconds.

Remove dough from the oil and place on a sheet tray. Top with marinara sauce and cheese. Place the pizza under the broiler for 2 minutes until crust is bubbly and charred. Top with a generous amount of basil, a sprinkle of salt and a drizzle of olive oil.

Mushroom Flatbread
MAKES 1 PIE

Grilled pizza has a wonderful texture – half bagel, half pizza. Using a grill creates a slightly charred and crispy outside while keeping the inside chewy and sweet. Grilled flatbread also works for sandwiches.

1 pizza dough (page 21)
1 1/2 tablespoons extra virgin olive oil, divided
3 cups assorted mushrooms, roughly chopped
1 teaspoon fine sea salt, divided
3 tablespoons dry red wine
1 tablespoon unsalted butter
1 cup fresh ricotta cheese (page 29)
1 cup chives, finely chopped

Heat grill pan or grill to medium high heat and form pizza dough into desired shape. Set aside.

In a skillet heat 1/2 tablespoon of olive oil over medium high heat and place 1 cup of the mushrooms in the pan at a time. Allow mushrooms to brown on one side before stirring. Stir mushrooms and season with 1/3 teaspoon of salt. Add about 1 tablespoon of wine and allow it to burn off. Finish with a touch of butter. Repeat for all mushrooms, using the remaining olive oil, salt, wine and butter.

Place raw dough on the grill and cook until slightly charred, 1 - 2 minutes per side. Remove from the grill and top with mushrooms and cheese. Garnish with chives.

dinner with friends

There's nothing like a cozy night in with a few good friends, a couple bottles of wine and fabulous food. That's my kind of night.

STUFFED ARTICHOKES

———

SMASHED POTATOES & BLUE CHEESE BUTTER

———

CROSTINI

———

RARE ROAST BEEF

———

ROASTED CAULIFLOWER

———

APPLE TARTE TATIN

Stuffed Artichokes

SERVES 4 - 6

Artichokes mystify people – and it's not surprising. The best advice I can give you? YouTube it! Look up how to prep an artichoke, follow this recipe and you're in business.

4 whole artichokes
1 lemon, halved
2 teaspoons fine sea salt, divided
1 cup panko
4 tablespoons unsalted butter, cubed
2 - 3 tablespoons extra virgin olive oil
1 cup chopped parsley
1 cup grated Parmesan cheese

Preheat broiler. Cut bottom and top off artichokes. Remove outer more fibrous leaves from the artichoke. Rub the cut side of the lemon on the cut areas of the artichoke. Place the artichokes bottom side down in a pasta pot. Fill the pot with 2 - 3" water. Place the halved lemon in pot and bring to a boil, season with 1 teaspoon salt.

Cover and steam artichokes until tender, about 35 minutes, or until the leaves easily pull away. Remove the artichokes and allow them to cool completely.

Combine panko, butter, olive oil, parsley, cheese and remaining teaspoon of salt until it resembles a crumble. Stuff leaves of the artichoke evenly with the crumble.

Place on a baking sheet and broil until browned and crispy. Serve while warm.

To eat pull leaves out of the choke and eat the bottom of the leaf. When you reach the center, eat the heart in its entirety.

Smashed Potatoes with Blue Cheese Butter

SERVES 4 - 6

This is the perfect potato side, satisfying lovers of both "crispy" and "gooey" potatoes. These smashed potatoes are crunchy on the outside and soft on the inside. P.S. Salt is their best friend.

1 stick unsalted butter, room temperature
2 - 3 ounces blue cheese
1 lb. small waxy round potatoes (any color)
Fine sea salt
Extra virgin olive oil, as needed
1 bunch chives, finely chopped

Whip or mash butter with blue cheese and roll into a 1" log using plastic wrap or parchment paper. Chill in the refrigerator until set. Butter can also be frozen for up to 3 months.

Preheat oven to 200° F.

Wash potatoes and place in a large pot of cold water. Bring to a boil and season with salt. Reduce the heat and simmer, cooking until potatoes are fork-tender, about 15 minutes. Remove the potatoes from the water and set aside to cool.

Using the heal of your hand, smash potatoes. In a large skillet heat 1 tablespoon olive oil over medium high heat. Arrange the potatoes in one layer to avoid overcrowding and cook until crispy, 3 - 4 minutes. Flip and crisp other side. Remove the poatoes and keep warm in a low oven. It is best to work in batches.

Slice butter over potatoes and garnish with chives.

crostini party

Basic Crostini
MAKES 2 DOZEN CROSTINI

Crostini is a perfect start to any party. Each of these recipes can top 1 dozen crostini, but feel free to mix and match.

1 baguette, cut into 1/4" thick slices
Extra virgin olive oil, as needed
1 - 2 garlic cloves, whole

Preheat oven to 350° F. Place baguette slices in a single layer on a sheet tray and drizzle or brush generously with olive oil. Cook until toasted, about 8 minutes. Remove and rub with garlic clove to infuse garlic flavor.

Cherry Tomato Crostini
MAKES 1/2 PINT

1 tablespoon extra virgin olive oil
1 pint cherry tomatoes
2 cloves garlic, whole
1 teaspoon fine sea salt
1 teaspoon sugar

Preheat oven to 325° F. On a sheet tray toss together olive oil, tomatoes, garlic, salt and sugar. Cook for 35 - 40 minutes, shaking the pan every 15 minutes or so until tomatoes begin to pop but don't lose their shape completely. Remove and discard garlic cloves. Place tomatoes in a bowl and stir to combine, adding more olive oil as desired.

Pear and Goat Cheese Crostini

1 - 2 ounces goat cheese, room temperature
1/2 pear, thinly sliced
1 tablespoon lemon juice
1/4 teaspoon fine sea salt
2 - 3 tablespoons toasted hazelnuts, roughly chopped

Spread crostini with goat cheese. Toss pears with lemon juice and salt. Top crostini with pears and hazelnuts.

Mushroom Crostini

1 cup assorted mushrooms, cooked
1 - 2 sprigs thyme
1 tablespoon lemon zest
Maldon sea salt
Extra virgin olive oil

Top crostini with mushrooms and season with thyme, zest and salt. Drizzle with olive oil.

Asparagus and Bacon Crostini

2 - 3 ounces blue cheese
6 slices bacon, cooked
10 - 12 asparagus, blanched
Extra virgin olive oil

Top crostini with blue cheese, then bacon and asparagus. Drizzle with olive oil if desired.

Ricotta and Radish Crostini

1 cup ricotta cheese (page 29)
3 - 4 radishes, thinly sliced
Maldon sea salt

Slather ricotta on crostini and top with sliced radishes. Season with salt.

Avocado Crostini

1 avocado
1 tablespoon lemon juice
1/2 teaspoon fine sea salt
1 tablespoon red pepper flakes
Extra virgin olive oil

Cut avocado in half and remove pit. Cut into large slices and toss with lemon juice, salt and red pepper flakes. Top crostini and finish with a drizzle of olive oil. Serve immediately to prevent oxidation.

Rare Roast Beef

SERVES 12

This is great buffet piece that can be served warm, cold or thinly sliced for a sandwich bar. Take the liberty and use whatever herbs you have on hand. Avoid using strong herbs (rosemary, cilantro, oregano) together, let one strong herb dominate and compliment with 2 - 3 milder herbs (dill, chive, parsley).

1 1/2 pounds beef rib eye roast, excess fat trimmed
1 cup mixed herbs: rosemary, thyme, parsley
Zest and juice 1 lemon
1 tablespoon fine sea salt
1/2 cup extra virgin olive oil
4 - 5 cloves garlic, whole
1 tablespoon vegetable oil
Maldon salt, garnish

Preheat oven to 450° F. Remove beef from refrigerator and allow it to temper at least 1 hour before roasting.

Chop herbs and mix with lemon juice, zest, salt and olive oil. Using a knife, stud the beef and insert garlic cloves into the meat.

Preheat vegetable oil in a high-sided ovenproof pan over high heat. Sear meat until browned on all sides, about 3 - 4 minutes per side. Remove from heat and place in the oven. Cook for additional 20 minutes or until the internal temperature of the beef reads 115° F. Transfer beef to a cutting board and tent the meat with tinfoil, rest for 20 minutes.

Thinly slice against the grain and season with Maldon salt.

Whole Roasted Cauliflower & Whipped Goat Cheese
SERVES 4 - 6

This is a show stopping side for vegetarians and carnivores alike. Slice thick and serve with a steak knife, it is sure to impress cauliflower virgins.

Roasted Cauliflower

1 head cauliflower, whole with leaves trimmed
1/2 bottle dry white wine
2 teaspoon fine sea salt, divided
Juice of 1 lemon
2 tablespoons unsalted butter
1 tablespoon crushed red pepper flakes
1 bay leaf
1 - 2 tablespoons extra virgin olive oil

Heat oven to 400° F.

Bring wine, salt, lemon juice, butter, red pepper flakes, bay leaf and 1 cup water to a boil in a medium high-sided pot and then remove from heat.

Rub olive oil over cauliflower and season with remaining salt. Place cauliflower in the pot. Place the pot in the oven and roast for 30 - 40 minutes until cauliflower is fork-tender and brown on top. For an extra char, heat the broiler to high and cook for an additional 3 - 4 minutes. Watch carefully to avoid burning.

Transfer cauliflower to a plate, drizzle with olive oil and sprinkle with sea salt. Serve with whipped goat cheese.

Whipped Goat Cheese

4 ounces fresh goat cheese
1/4 cup heavy cream
2 tablespoons olive oil, plus extra for garnish

Mix goat cheese and heavy cream, season with sea salt. Transfer whipped goat cheese to a serving bowl.

Apple Tarte Tatin

MAKES 1 TART

Oven to table, flip and plate for a perfect, "Ta-da!"

4 firm apples, peeled, halved and cored
4 tablespoons unsalted butter
1/4 cup sugar
1 teaspoon fine sea salt
1/2 teaspoon ground cinnamon
Pinch freshly grated nutmeg
1 frozen puff pastry, thawed
Whipped cream (page 80)

Preheat oven to 425° F.

Heat butter in a large ovenproof skillet. When melted add apples cut side down. Add sugar and continue to cook until underside of apples are slightly browned.

Flip apples and add the remaining seasoning. Remove from heat and cool. Roll puff pastry out to size of skillet and place on top of apples, tucking underneath the apples (not the pan) as needed. Place pan in the oven and bake 10 - 12 minutes, beginning to check around the 8 minute mark, until crust is golden brown.

To remove tart, flip onto a plate and serve with whipped cream or ice cream.

tailgating

PULLED PORK, BBQ SAUCE & PICKLED FENNEL

———

CARROTS WITH PESTO

———

OKTOBERFEST PRETZELS & HOMEMADE MUSTARD

———

ONE PAN BROWNIES

———

Pulled Pork
SERVES 12

I love pulled pork. A staple at southern tailgates (where a hog is often roasted whole and then butchered) that can be replicated at home. Check out my simple sauce below or use store bought sauce in a pinch. Pork butt (which is actually a cut from the pig's shoulder) is king for this, but feel free to use the remaining tenderloin from page 11 (they generally come in packs of 2).

1 3 lb. pork butt, excess fat trimmed
4 cups (1 quart) barbeque sauce, plus extra as needed
1 beer, pick your favorite

Preheat oven to 300° F. In an ovenproof pot place pork fat side up and pour barbeque sauce and beer over. Cover and cook for 3 hours, or until the meat is tender and pulls apart easily with two forks.

Remove pork from the oven and using two forks, shred the meat. Dress generously with extra sauce to create a well dressed pulled pork. Serve on buns with slaw, or naked with baked beans.

Fennel and Red Onion Slaw
MAKES 1 PINT

1 fennel bulb, halved and thinly sliced
1/2 red onion, thinly sliced
1 tablespoon fine sea salt
1 tablespoon honey
2 cloves garlic, whole
1 tablespoon whole cloves
1/2 cup apple cider vinegar
2 cups water

Place fennel and onion in a large bowl. Bring remaining ingredients to a simmer and pour over fennel mixture. Allow the mixture to cool. Use immediately or refrigerate for up to 1 week.

Basic Barbeque Sauce
MAKES 1 QUART

Everyone needs a BBQ sauce recipe. Just think of it as a tangy, southern marinara.

1 tablespoon vegetable oil
1 sweet onion, finely chopped
3 gloves garlic, finely chopped
1 cup ketchup
1 cup crushed canned tomatoes
1/2 cup light brown sugar
1 teaspoon dry mustard
1 tablespoon fine sea salt
1 cup water
1 tablespoon unsulphured molasses
¼ cup apple cider vinegar

Heat oil in a medium saucepan. Cook onion over low heat until translucent, 8 - 10 minutes. Stir in garlic and cook until fragrant. Add remaining ingredients. Simmer over low heat for 30 minutes to fully develop the flavors.

Roasted Carrots with Parsley Sauce

SERVES 4

Update your crudité platter with these decidedly unfussy baby carrots. Simply roast them the day before the big game and transport. Drizzle sauce or use to dip.

1 bunch small carrots, peeled, tops reserved
1/2 cup plus 1 tablespoon extra virgin olive oil, divided
1/2 teaspoon fine sea salt
1/4 teaspoon paprika
1/4 teaspoon chili powder
1/4 teaspoon ground turmeric
1 shallot, minced
1 cup finely chopped herbs; dill, parsley and carrot tops

Preheat oven to 425° F. Toss carrots with 1 tablespoon olive oil, salt and spices. Roast for 10 - 15 minutes, until just tender but still somewhat al dente.

Combine shallot, herbs and remaining olive oil together. Drizzle over carrots.

Homemade Pretzels
MAKES 8

Pretzels may not be standard tailgate fare (at least not yet!), but this Oktoberfest favorite fits right into your fall schedule. The dough, similar to that of a bagel is easy to make in a stand mixer, and since you already have that bread flour from the Classic Pizza Dough (page 21), you might as well.

1 3/4 cup warm water, 110° F
1 tablespoon sugar
1 tablespoon fine sea salt
1 3/4 teaspoon active dry yeast
4 3/4 cup bread flour
2 tablespoons unsalted butter, softened
1/2 cup baking soda
1 egg yolk, whisked
Pretzel salt and poppy seed, garnish

Combine water, sugar, salt and yeast. Allow the mixture to sit for 5 minutes. In a stand mixer fitted with a hook attachment combine flour and yeast mixture. Mix on the lowest speed until the dough begins to come together, add 1 tablespoon of butter at a time. Knead until smooth.

Remove dough from the bowl. Spray the bowl with cooking spray and place the dough back into the bowl. Allow the mixture to rise for 3 - 4 hours, until the dough doubles in size.

Preheat oven to 450° F.

Cut dough into 8 equal portions and roll into long rods, about 20" - 22" long. Fold each into a pretzel shape.

Meanwhile, bring 1 quart water to a boil and add baking soda. Simmer each pretzel for 30 seconds, remove and place pretzels on a sheet tray to dry.

Brush each pretzel with egg yolk and sprinkle with salt, poppy seeds or both. Bake for 17 - 20 minutes until pretzels are golden brown. Serve with mustard.

Whole Grain Mustard

1/4 cup yellow mustard seeds
1/4 cup brown mustard seeds
1/3 cup champagne vinegar
1 teaspoon fine sea salt
1/2 teaspoon finely ground pepper

Combine all ingredients and allow the mixture to sit overnight. For smoother mustard, puree until desired consistency is reached.

One Pan Brownies
MAKES ONE 6 X 6 TRAY OF BROWNIES

This recipe is fabulous because it only involves one pan and one spoon. Stove-to-oven-to-mouth in less than 30 minutes. Now, take *that* to the game.

1 stick unsalted butter, room temperature
1 cup chocolate chips
1 teaspoon vanilla extract
1 teaspoon fine sea salt
2 eggs
1/2 cup sugar
1/3 cup all-purpose flour
1/3 cup whole raw walnuts

Preheat oven to 325° F.

Over low heat, slowly warm a metal brownie pan or small cast iron skillet (do not use a glass pan for this) to melt butter and chocolate, stirring until just melted. Remove pan from the burner and add vanilla, salt and one egg at a time.

As the batter thickens add sugar and flour, stirring until just combined.

Wipe sides of the tray or skillet (for clean edges) and stud the surface with walnuts. Place brownies in the oven and bake for 20 - 22 minutes or until the brownie is set, but slightly gooey. A knife inserted in the center of the pan should have moist crumbs upon removal.

Cool completely and serve.

ladies who lunch

There's no way I'm "lunching" on a daily basis – although I wish I was. Not only is lunch my favorite meal, but it's often the least appreciated. It's important to put thought and energy into the midday meal!

BASIC GREENS & DRESSING

———

FARRO AND BUTTERNUT SQUASH SALAD

———

ROASTED BEET SALAD

———

WARM HERB POTATO SALAD

———

TOMATO SALAD

———

Basic Greens & Dressing
MAKES ABOUT 1 CUP DRESSING

If everyone stopped buying bottled salad dressing, the world would be a better place. All dressing requires is acid (vinegar or lemon), salt and fat (olive oil, mayo, canola oil, yogurt, etc.). Once you understand this concept your pantry will seem like an endless supply of dressing ideas.

1 shallot, minced
Juice of 1 lemon
1 teaspoon fine sea salt
1/4 cup whole grain mustard
1/2 cup of extra virgin olive oil
Greens, washed and dried thoroughly

In a small bowl combine shallot, lemon juice and salt. Allow the mixture to sit for 5 minutes and macerate. This lessens the pungency of the shallot. Stir in mustard. Slowly whisk in olive oil, until the dressing is emulsified.

Toasted Farro Salad
SERVES 4 - 6

Farro, a fabulous little nutty grain from Italy (high in fiber and protein) is the new quinoa. Toasting before simmering boosts flavor. Toss with any vegetable (roasted or not), herb or cheese you have on hand. Serve hot or cold – it's that good.

1 butternut squash, peeled and diced
4 tablespoons extra virgin olive oil, divided
Fine sea salt, to taste
1/2 lb. dry farro
1 quart chicken or vegetable stock
1 cup hazelnuts, toasted and chopped
Juice of 1 lemon
1 bunch parsley, chopped
1 bunch chives, chopped

Preheat oven to 425° F.

Lay squash in one layer on a sheet tray. Toss with 2 tablespoons olive oil and season with salt. Roast 20 - 25 minutes until golden brown. Set aside to cool.

In a large pot add 1 tablespoon olive oil and toast farro until slightly browned and fragrant. Add stock and bring to a simmer. Cover and simmer lightly until farro is al dente, 20 - 25 minutes. Drain and set aside in a large bowl. Add squash, hazelnuts, lemon juice and remaining 1 tablespoon olive oil. Season with salt as needed.

Top with parsley and chives.

Roasted Beet Salad with Whipped Goat Cheese
SERVES 4

3 large red beets
1 tablespoon red wine vinegar
2 tablespoons extra virgin olive oil, divided
2 teaspoons fine sea salt
Juice and zest of 1 lemon
Whipped goat cheese (page 44)
1 bunch watercress, roughly chopped
Maldon salt, garnish

Preheat oven to 375° F degrees.

Wash and trim beets. Season with vinegar, 1 tablespoon olive oil and 1 teaspoon salt. Wrap in tinfoil and place beets on a sheet tray. Roast beets until tender and can be easily pierced with a knife, about 1 - 1 1/2 hours. Remove beets from the oven and peel. Cut into 1" pieces and toss with remaining salt, olive oil and lemon zest and juice.

Plate beets and garnish with cheese, watercress and Maldon salt.

Warm Herb Potato Salad
SERVES 4

I'm not a fan of mayo so this is how I roll with potato salad. Perfect for a spring brunch, weekday lunch or buffet.

1 lb. baby potatoes or fingerling potatoes
2 cloves garlic, minced
1/2 cup whole grain mustard
1/4 - 1/2 cup extra virgin olive oil
1 cup chopped fresh herbs: thyme, tarragon, dill and chives
2 - 3 tablespoons capers, drained and finely chopped
Fine sea salt, to taste

Place potatoes in a large pot of cold water and bring to a boil. Salt the water generously and cook until fork-tender. Remove potatoes from the pot and allow them to cool slightly. If needed, cut potatoes into bite size pieces. Place potatoes in a large bowl and toss with garlic, mustard, olive oil, herbs and capers.

Drizzle with additional olive oil and season with salt, to taste.

Heirloom Tomato Salad
SERVES 8

It's silly that this is even a recipe but I can't leave out my very favorite salad. Only make this in July and August, otherwise you'll be sorely disappointed. Just like waiting all year for Thanksgiving fare, tomatoes are equally requited and savored during summer.

3 lb. heirloom tomatoes, sliced thick
Extra virgin olive oil
Fine sea salt, to taste
Maldon salt, to taste

Lay tomatoes out on large serving tray and generously drizzle with olive oil and sprinkle with salt. When serving finish with Maldon salt.

bubbly brunch

Brunch is breakfast + lunch, on steroids. Most chefs hate it. Everyone else, well, let's just say it's what weekends are made of. Eggs, cheese and a meal where both booze and eating dessert before the meal are not only acceptable, but encouraged, is always okay in my book.

LEMON POPPY SEED BREAD

———

POACHED EGGS WITH HOLLANDAISE

———

SHRIMP AND GRITS

———

CHOCOLATE SCONES WITH JAM

———

CITRUS SALAD

———

Lemon Poppy Seed Bread

MAKES 1 BUNDT CAKE

I have a girl crush on anything lemon/poppy seed. This recipe is perfect for someone who enjoys eating dessert all day long (me!) because it's just sweet enough to feel like you're indulging but light enough to have for breakfast or an afternoon snack. Think pound cake, but lighter.

2 1/2 cups all-purpose flour
2 teaspoons baking powder
1/2 teaspoon fine sea salt
1 cup vegetable oil
1 cup sugar
2 large eggs
1 cup evaporated milk
1/3 cup milk
1 tablespoon vanilla extract
Juice and zest of 1 lemon, divided
1/4 cup poppy seeds
1/2 cup powdered sugar

Preheat oven to 350° F. Spray a bundt pan with cooking spray.

In a large bowl, sift together flour, baking powder, and salt. Set aside.

In another large bowl, mix oil and sugar. Add the eggs one at a time, beating well after each addition until the mixture is fully incorporated. Add the evaporated milk, milk and vanilla. Add dry ingredients and mix well. Stir in lemon zest, 1 tablespoon lemon juice and poppy seeds.

Bake for 40 - 45 minutes or until a cake tester comes out with moist crumbs. Let the cake cool for 20 minutes in the bundt pan. Remove from the pan before serving.

To make lemon icing, combine remaining 1 tablespoon lemon juice with powdered sugar and whisk until there are no lumps and sugar is moist. Drizzle over cake and allow it to harden.

Tip: Evaporated milk is a shelf-stable milk product that's had about half its water content removed. It is not the same as sweetened condensed milk, which has added sugar. Don't attempt to substitute regular milk or sweetened condensed milk for this.

Poached Eggs
MAKES 6 EGGS

Poached eggs scare people and they shouldn't. Prep ahead (yep, you can do this) and reheat in a water bath, in a low oven, for the perfect no fuss brunch that will make you look like a superstar.

1 tablespoon fine sea salt
1 teaspoon white wine vinegar
6 eggs
Extra virgin olive oil

Bring a pot of water to a boil, season with salt and vinegar. Crack egg and place in a tiny ramekin.

Slowly drop one egg at a time into the water, positioning the ramekin as close to the water as possible. Cover and allow the egg to boil for 2 minutes. Remove the egg with a slotted spoon and place on a paper towel to dry. Trim excess white and place on a baking sheet drizzled with olive oil. Repeat with the remaining eggs.

These can be kept warm in a 200° F oven until you're ready to serve them.

If you're not planning to serve immediately, remove eggs from the pot and place in an ice bath to stop cooking. Eggs can be made the night before, kept in an ice bath in the refrigerator and reheated in a low oven.

For a smaller pot, don't attempt more than 1 - 2 eggs per batch. This may seem tedious but it'll prevent the egg whites from wrapping up in each other or breaking the yolks.

Chive Hollandaise
MAKES 1 CUP

Hollandaise uses the same technique as homemade mayo but with butter. It is the ultimate breakfast sauce. The trick is fresh room temperature eggs.

1 egg yolk, room temperature
1 tablespoon lemon juice
1/2 teaspoon fine sea salt
1 stick unsalted butter (1/2 cup), melted and cooled
1 tablespoon chopped chives

In a metal bowl place egg yolk, lemon juice and salt.

Over a double boiler heat egg yolk for 1 minute, whisking continuously until just warmed.

Remove eggs from heat and slowly whisk in melted butter, a drop at a time, until an emulsified sauce forms that is thick and creamy.

Add chives and season with salt, if needed.

Shrimp and Grits
SERVES 4

Shrimps and grits are a staple in the South and everyone has their own recipe. I have a secret; grits are polenta (I'm talking to you Italians!) so the same principles apply. You can easily substitute one for the other if you can't find grits at the store (see page 11). Feel free to use whatever water-to-grits ratio you please. I've found a good ratio for the home cook is 4:1, 4 cups liquid to 1 cup grits.

4 - 5 cups of liquid, such as water, broth, milk, cream or a combination
1 cup of grits (not instant)
1 - 2 teaspoons fine sea salt, divided
4 tablespoons unsalted butter
1/2 - 1 cup of cheddar cheese, shredded
15 - 20 medium sized shrimp, peeled and deveined
1/2 teaspoon cayenne pepper
4 strips of bacon, chopped
1 onion, diced
2 gloves garlic, minced
1 jalapeno pepper, seeds removed and minced
1/2 cup of white wine
Chopped parsley, garnish

Heat liquid in a large pot. Bring to a boil and add grits while whisking. Whisk frequently over medium low heat until grits absorb the liquid and begin to thicken.

Season with salt, butter and cheese. Keep warm and fluid, adding more liquid if needed.

Place shrimp in a bowl and season with salt and cayenne.

Meanwhile cook bacon over medium heat until browned. Remove bacon from the pan and drain on a paper towel. To remaining bacon fat, add onion to the pan and sauté until translucent, about 5 minutes. Add garlic and jalapeno and cook until fragrant, about 1 minute. Add shrimp and cook for 1 - 2 minutes per side, until light pink.

Add wine to deglaze the pan, scrapping the brown bits off the bottom. Allow the shrimp mixture to thicken slightly and remove from the heat.

Plate the grits and top with shrimp. Garnish with extra cheddar and parsley.

Chocolate Scones

MAKES 8 SCONES

Scones are like biscuits, but with sugar. Using what's known as the "cut-in butter method" you'll splinter cold butter into the flour until it resembles a coarse meal. If butter becomes warm during the process, the refrigerator is your friend to rechill the butter. The secret to flakey, light scones (and biscuits for that matter) is cold butter + hot oven.

2 1/2 cups all-purpose flour
1/4 cup sugar, additional for garnish
2 teaspoons baking powder
1/2 teaspoon baking soda
1/2 teaspoon fine sea salt
1 stick unsalted butter, cubed and chilled
1 cup buttermilk
1 egg plus 1 yolk, divided
1/2 cup chocolate chunks
1 tablespoon water

Tip: Less is more for scones, don't overmix!

Preheat oven to 425° F. Line a sheet tray with parchment paper and set aside.

In large bowl, whisk together flour, sugar, baking powder, baking soda, and salt. Using a pastry cutter, or two forks, break butter into the flour until crumbly. Make a well in the flour mixture and add egg, buttermilk and chocolate chips.

Using a fork lightly "toss" until a shaggy dough forms. It will not look like traditional dough, which is ideal!

Place dough onto a floured surface and press into a square about 3/4" in thickness. Cut into 8 scones and place on the sheet tray.

To make egg wash whisk together the remaining yolk with 1 tablespoon water. Brush on scones and sprinkle with sugar. Bake until golden, 12 - 15 minutes. Cool on a wire rack before serving.

Serve with jam.

Easy Mixed Berry Jam

MAKES 1 PINT

Jam is relaxing to make. Wash berries, sort through and discard blistered, bruised or moldy berries. Toss with sugar, lemon and salt. If you're feeling crafty, jar and store for winter.

3 pints mixed berries, washed and picked through
2 cups sugar
1 lemon, juiced

Place all ingredients in a saucepan and simmer over low heat for 1 hour. Pour into jars for canning or keep refrigerated in air tight container for up to 2 weeks.

Citrus Salad with Pistachio Dressing

SERVES 4

This everyday citrus salad will make you look like Martha Stewart. It's all about cutting the citrus correctly.

1 grapefruit
1 cara cara orange
1 Florida orange
1 meyer lemon
1 lime
1/4 cup honey
1 teaspoon sugar
1/4 teaspoon fine sea salt
1/4 cup toasted and chopped pistachios
1/2 cup mint

With a sharp knife cut both ends of each fruit off, giving yourself two flat surfaces. Working slowly cut downwards, from one flat surface to the other, removing the skin. Then slice each piece of citrus into 1/4" rounds.

Place citrus on a larger platter. Drizzle with honey and sprinkle with sugar, salt, pistachios and mint.

treat yo' self

We all know that dessert is the best part of any meal. As a self-proclaimed "sweet tooth" I wait all meal for this satisfying end. Chocolate, sugar, icing or cream, this is by far the best part of my meal. Treat yo' self.

BIRTHDAY CAKE

———

PAVLOVA

———

MEYER LEMON TART

———

FLOURLESS CHOCOLATE CAKE

———

CHOCOLATE MOUSSE

———

Birthday Cake

MAKES 2, 9" CAKES

People fall into two categories: butter cake lovers and oil cake lovers. If you find yourself a fan of light boxed cakes (guilty) you most likely enjoy baked goods with oil. Prefer a dense rich cake? Butter cake is your jam and this recipe will be your next birthday cake. The trick is whipping the butter and sugar together for a long time, at least 5 minutes. And the milk chocolate icing is a nice throwback to childhood.

4 cups all-purpose flour
2 teaspoons baking powder
1 teaspoon baking soda
1 teaspoon salt
2 sticks unsalted butter, at room temperature
2 cups sugar
1 teaspoon vanilla extract
4 eggs
2 cups buttermilk

Preheat oven to 350° F. Butter two 9" round cake pans and line the bottoms of the pans with circles of parchment paper, then butter the parchment.

Whisk together flour, baking powder, baking soda, and salt in a medium bowl.

In a stand mixer, fitted with a paddle attachment, whip butter and sugar until light and fluffy, at least 5 minutes. Add vanilla. Add one egg at a time, beating really well after each addition. The mixture should not "break" its emulsion. If it does, crank up the speed and beat until it returns. A stand or hand mixer can be used.

Add flour mixture and milk all at once and mix. Traditional recipes generally call for alternating these two, which often leads to overmixing. Pour batter into cake pans and bake until set and a toothpick inserted in the center comes out slightly crumbly, 30 - 35 minutes. Cool completely before icing.

Milk Chocolate Icing

1 lb. milk chocolate, melted and cooled
1 teaspoon vanilla extract
1 1/2 - 2 cups crème fraiche or sour cream, room temperature

Using a rubber spatula mix all ingredients together until you reach the desired consistency. For a thicker fudge-like icing use less crème fraiche. Cover and chill.

Ice cake and chill cake to set. Remove 10 - 15 minutes before cutting and serving.

Tip: The key to this icing is making sure both the melted chocolate and crème fraiche are the same temperature, room temperature. If the chocolate is even slightly warm it will melt the crème fraiche and never set.

Pavlova

MAKES 1 LARGE PAVLOVA

I call Pavlova a "big marshmallow" because it's light, shiny and gorgeous – just like the Russian ballerina it was named for. A stunning end to dinner parties, use any berry or fruit to make your compote.

6 egg whites
1 pinch fine sea salt
1 teaspoon vanilla extract
1/2 teaspoon cream of tartar
1 tablespoon cornstarch
1 cup sugar

Place rack in the middle of the oven and preheat oven to 250° F. Line a large baking sheet with parchment.

In a stand mixer fitted with whisk attachment, whip egg whites until just frothy. Add salt, vanilla extract, cream of tartar and cornstarch. Slowly add sugar and beat until meringue is shiny and stiff peaks form.

Pour onto baking sheet and make a slight well in the center; this is where berry compote will go. Bake until dry, about 1 hour and remove from the oven. Cool and top with compote.

Tip: Cream of tartar and corn starch are two stabilizers used to create a meringue. If you don't have, don't worry, just make sure to pay particular attention not to over-whip the whites.

Blackberry Compote

2 pints blackberries
1/2 cup sugar
1/2 teaspoon fine sea salt
1 lemon, juiced

In a small saucepan over low heat, combine all ingredients and bring to a simmer. Cook, stirring occasionally, until the berries begin to break down and the sauce is slightly thickened.

Meyer Lemon Tart
MAKES 2, 9" TARTS

This recipe calls for lots of eggs, sorry chickens. Save extra curd for toast, scones (page 70) or crepes. Meyer lemons are in season during late winter but regular lemons will work just fine too.

Crust

2 cups all-purpose flour
1 tablespoon sugar
2 sticks unsalted butter, cubed and chilled
2 eggs
1/4 cup cold water

Lemon Curd

10 egg yolks
1 cup sugar
6 meyer lemons, zested and juiced
4 tablespoons unsalted butter, cubed
Powdered sugar, to finish

In a food processor or large bowl combine flour and sugar. Add butter and pulse or break using a fork until butter is the size of lentils. In a small bowl, whisk water and eggs. Slowly stream mixture into the flour mixture and mix just until the dough comes together. Divide into two disks and chill for at least 30 minutes.

Preheat oven to 425° F.

On a floured surface, roll both doughs into 10" circles. Place in two pie or tart pans and poke the bottoms with a fork. Prebake the shells until lightly browned and completely dry, about 12 - 15 minutes. Remove the shells and allow them to cool completely.

Meanwhile combine eggs, sugar, zest, and lemon juice in bowl over a double boiler and whisk continuously until the mixture begins to thicken, this will take about 10 minutes. It will be very thick, like pudding. Remove from heat and add butter. Pass through a fine mesh strainer to remove any bits of cooked egg.

Fill the crusts with lemon curd and chill for at least 30 minutes. When ready to serve, dust with powdered sugar.

You can also make 1 tart and freeze extra dough and curd for a later use.

Tip: This lemon curd also works as a great substitute for jam when spreading on toast or filling cookies.

Flourless Chocolate Cake

MAKES 1 CAKE

This cake was trendy before gluten-free was "in." Flourless chocolate cake is rich, fudgy and dense. Undercook it just slightly.

1 lb. dark chocolate, chopped
1 stick unsalted butter, diced
2 tablespoons vegetable oil
6 large eggs, separated
1/2 cup sugar, divided
2 tablespoons unsweetened cocoa powder
1 teaspoon fine sea salt
1 teaspoon vanilla

Preheat oven to 350° F.

Lightly butter a 9" springform or cake pan and then line with parchment paper. Combine chocolate, oil and butter in a small bowl and place over a double boiler. Melt and remove from heat, allowing the mixture to cool slightly.

In a small bowl, whisk egg yolks, 1/4 cup sugar and cocoa powder. Slowly combine the egg and melted chocolate, whisk until smooth.

In a stand mixer (or with a hand mixer), whisk egg whites, salt and remaining sugar until light, fluffy and stiff peaks form. "Sacrifice" a bit of the whites and lighten the chocolate mixture. Add remaining meringue and fold into chocolate to avoid deflating.

Pour the batter into the cake pan and bake until the top is dry and just set, 35 - 40 minutes. Allow the cake to cool slightly and remove from the cake pan.

Cool on a wire rack and top with whipped cream before serving.

Whipped Cream

1 cup heavy cream
2 tablespoons crème fraiche

Whip heavy cream and crème fraiche in a stand mixer fitted with a whisk attachement until a soft peaks form.

Chocolate Mousse

I love this recipe because it makes the world's richest mousse and combines two of my favorite egg techniques: pâte à bombe (whipped egg yolks and sugar) and meringue (whipped egg whites and sugar). There are three important steps (and a set of dishes), but it's worth it. If you want to make the recipe easier (or create a lighter mousse), simply omit the pâte à bombe and fold meringue into the chocolate.

1 lb. dark chocolate, chopped
1 stick of unsalted butter
6 large eggs, separated
1 teaspoon fine sea salt
4 tablespoons sugar, divided
Whipped cream (page 80)

Over a double boiler, warm the chocolate and the butter over medium heat, stirring occasionally until just melted. Let cool slightly.

In a stand mixer fitted with a whisk attachment or with a hand mixer, whisk egg whites, salt and 2 tablespoons sugar until stiff peaks form. Set aside.

In a second bowl, whisk egg yolks and remaining sugar until pale yellow, about 5 minutes. Slowly whisk in chocolate mixture until just combined. "Sacrifice" a bit of the meringue to lighten the chocolate mixture. Then fold in meringue completely until there are no streaks. Cover and refrigerate for at least 1 hour.

Tip: This recipe calls for raw eggs, so use good eggs. If this scares you, gently warm the bottom of the bowl over the double boiler you're using for melting the chocolate until the eggs reach 145° F, whisking continually, before whipping the pâte à bombe or meringue.

bio

Ashton Keefe is a chef, culinary instructor and recipe developer in NYC. Ashton creates content for Whole Foods Market, Food 52, *O Magazine*, *Everyday with Rachael Ray*, *Real Simple*, *Cooking Light*, *People Magazine* and *Shape Magazine*. This is Ashton's first cookbook. Additional recipes, videos and services available at http://www.ashtonkeefe.com.

Acknowledgments

Thank you to all my teachers, students, mentors, editors and most importantly, taste testers who made this book and everyday in this business enjoyable and something I love.

Special thanks to Emily Brickel for The Style Line and FEED Super illustration, Karoline Engel, Cabell Belk, Laura Arnold, Kira Niesielowski, Sami Fox, Kristen Green, Peter Cornbrooks and most importantly my friends and family - my favorite guests and dining companions that define my everyday kitchen revelry.

CPSIA information can be obtained at www.ICGtesting.com
Printed in the USA
LVIW01n1428220415
435651LV00027B/150